EDGE BOOKS™

# THE KIDS' GUIDE TO

# SIGN LANGUAGE

by Kathryn Clay

**Consultant:**
Kari Sween
American Sign Language Instructor
Minnesota State University
Mankato, Minnesota

CAPSTONE PRESS
a capstone imprint

Edge Books are published by Capstone Press,
1710 Roe Crest Drive, North Mankato, Minnesota 56003.
www.capstonepub.com

*Library of Congress Cataloging-in-Publication Data*
Clay, Kathryn.
    The kids' guide to sign language / by Kathryn Clay.
    p. cm.—(Edge books. Kids' guides)
    Includes bibliographical references and index.
    Summary: "Step-by-step instructions show how to perform useful phrases using
American Sign Language"—Provided by publisher.
    ISBN 978-1-4296-8426-2 (library binding)
    ISBN 978-1-62065-230-5 (ebook PDF)
    1. Sign language—Juvenile literature. I. Title.
HV2476.C56 2013
419'.7—dc23

2011048908

**Editorial Credits**

Aaron Sautter, editor; Tracy McCabe, designer; Svetlana Zhurkin, media researcher;
    Laura Manthe, production specialist

**Photo Credits**

All photos by Capstone Studio/Karon Dubke except:
iStockphotos: Miodrag Nikolic, 7; Shutterstock: Diana Rich (pattern), cover
    and throughout, idea for life (background texture), cover and throughout,
    Terry Chan, cover (top), back cover (bottom)

Printed in the United States of America in North Mankato, Minnesota.
072018    000783

# Table of Contents

# COMMUNICATING
# WITH SIGNS

If you look around, you probably see people often using their hands to communicate. Football referees raise their hands in the air to signal a touchdown. Police officers put their hands out to stop cars.

People who are deaf or hard of hearing use their hands, faces, and bodies to communicate. These motions are called sign language.

In 1817 Thomas Hopkins Gallaudet and Laurent Clerc opened the American School for the Deaf in Hartford, Connecticut. Gallaudet and Clerc used signs they had learned in France to teach deaf students how to communicate. They combined the French signs with signs deaf people were already using to form American Sign Language (ASL). Since then, ASL has become the main form of communication for people who are deaf.

**FACT:**
American Sign Language is the fourth most common language used in the United States.

Is there a girl who is deaf at your school who you'd like to talk to? Or maybe a deaf boy just moved in down the street. Here's your chance to talk to them in sign language.

It's okay if you don't know the sign for every word. Remember that learning to sign is like learning any new language. It's important to practice often. After learning the basics, you'll find that signing is easy and fun!

## Spell It Out

The best signs to learn first are the letters of the alphabet. Once you know how to sign letters, you can spell out any word. This is called fingerspelling. Fingerspelling is most often used to sign names. But it's also handy if you don't know the sign for a certain word. You can just fingerspell it.

# ALPHABET

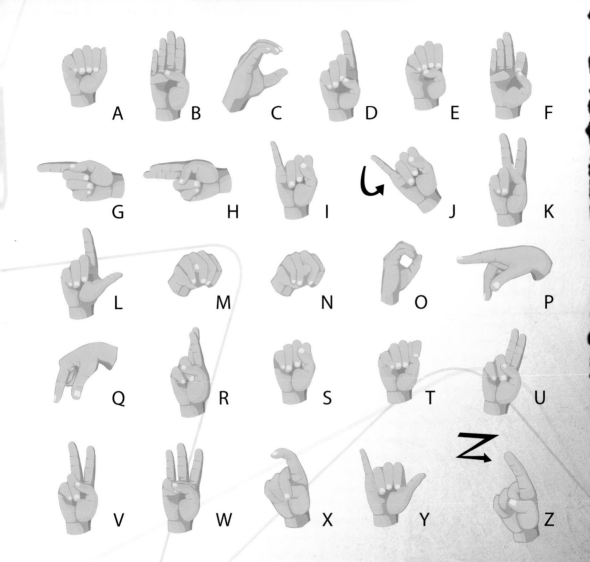

A B C D E F

G H I J K

L M N O P

Q R S T U

V W X Y Z

**FACT:**
Signs usually don't need to be done with a certain hand. Whether right-handed or left-handed, signers use whichever hand feels comfortable for most signs.

# 2 LEARNING THE BASICS

Fingerspelling is great to use if you don't know a word or two. But it's not easy to fingerspell a whole conversation. It's important to learn basic signs to quickly speak with a deaf person. Here are a few words and phrases to get you started.

## HELLO, WHAT'S YOUR NAME?

**Hello:** Wave your hand.

**Your:** Face your palm toward the other person.

**Name:** Make the "H" sign with both hands, and then tap your fingers together.

**What:** Place your hands at your sides with your palms facing up. Shrug your shoulders as you do this.

# MY NAME IS _ _ _ _ _ .

**My:** Place your palm to your chest.

**Name:** Make the "H" sign with both hands, and then tap your fingers together.

Fingerspell your name using the alphabet chart on page 7.

# NICE TO MEET YOU.

**Nice:** Slide the palm of one hand across the palm of your other hand.

**Meet:** Point up your index finger on both hands, and then touch your fingers together.

**You:** Point at the person you're talking to.

## YES

Make the "S" sign, and then move your wrist up and down.

## NO

Close your thumb and first two fingers together. Shake your head "no" as you do this.

## PLEASE

Place your palm on your chest and move in a circle.

## THANK YOU

Place your fingertips near your mouth. Then move your hand away from your mouth as if you're blowing a kiss.

## YOU'RE WELCOME

Reach out your hand with your palm face up. Then bring your hand inward toward your waist.

# GOOD MORNING, GOOD NIGHT

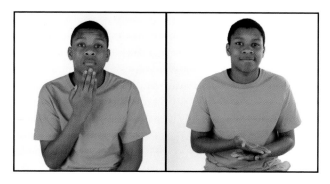

**Good:** Start with the "Thank you" sign. Then bring your hand down to rest in the palm of your other hand.

**Morning:** Cross your left arm in front of you. Arc your right hand and forearm up over left hand toward your body.

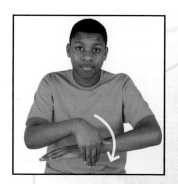

**Night:** Cross your left arm in front of you. Bend your right hand down and arc your right hand and forearm down across your left hand.

# ARE YOU OK?

**You:** Point at the person you are talking to.

**O:** Fingerspell the letter "O."

**K:** Fingerspell the letter "K."

# DO YOU NEED HELP?

**You:** Point at the person you are talking to.

**Need:** Fingerspell the letter "X," and then move your wrist in a downward motion.

**Help:** Make the letter "A" sign with one hand. Place this hand on the palm of the other hand, and then move both hands up.

# PLEASE HELP ME

**Please:** Place your palm on your chest and move your hand in a circle.

**Help:** Make the letter "A" sign with one hand. Place this hand on the palm of the other hand, and then move both hands up.

**Me:** Point to your chest.

# CONGRATULATIONS

Cup your hands together and shake forward once.

# SIGNING CAREFULLY

Be careful how you use your hands. Many signs look similar but have very different meanings. For example, it's easy to sign "toilet" by accident when you mean to sign "Tuesday."

**Tuesday**

**toilet**

# 3 SHARING YOUR FEELINGS

In many conversations, it's common to ask how the other person is feeling. In ASL facial expressions are an important part of sharing your feelings. Smiling, frowning, and rolling your eyes all show how you feel about something. Here are a few signs that you can use to help express your feelings and understand the feelings of others.

## HOW ARE YOU FEELING?

**How:** Cup both of your hands with knuckles touching. Keep your knuckles together and curve your hands down until your palms are face up.

**You:** Point at the person you're talking to.

**Feel:** Touch your chest with your middle finger. Move this finger up and away from your body.

# I FEEL _ _ _ _ _ _ _ _ .
## (EXCITED, HAPPY, ANGRY, SAD, TIRED, SCARED)

**Feel:** Touch your chest with your middle finger. Move your finger up and away from your body.

**I:** Point to your chest.

**Excited:** Touch your chest with the middle finger of each hand. Then quickly circle your hands in opposite directions two or three times.

**Happy:** Hold your hand at an upward angle. Then circle your hand twice in an upward motion.

**Angry:** Bend your fingers in front of your face. Then make an angry face while pulling your hand away.

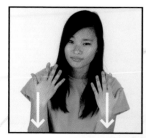

**Sad:** Place palms in front of your face. Then make a sad face as you move your hands downward.

**Tired:** Cup your hands on your chest. Then move your wrists downward and slump your shoulders like you're tired.

 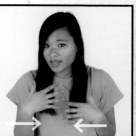

**Scared:** Place your fists at the sides of your chest. Then move your hands toward the center of your chest. Open your hands wide and make a scared face as you do this motion.

# 4 SIGNING AT SCHOOL

Is there a deaf boy or girl at your school? Keep reading to learn how to ask about her favorite class. Or learn how to invite him to join the football game at recess. The following signs will help you talk with deaf people you know at school.

## I HAVE A LOT OF HOMEWORK.

**I:** Point to your chest.

**A Lot:** Spread your fingers out on both hands in front of you. Then spread your arms out wide to your sides.

**Home:** Close your fingertips together on one hand and touch your chin. Then touch the top of your cheek.

**Work:** Form your hands into fists. Then tap the top fist on the bottom wrist with your hands facing down.

# I'M IN _ _ _ _ _ GRADE.
## (FIRST, SECOND, THIRD, FOURTH, FIFTH, SIXTH)

**I:** Point to your chest.

**Grade:** First form the letter "G" sign with one hand. Then bounce your hand two times on the open palm of your other hand.

**First:** Hold up your first finger.

**Second:** Hold up your first two fingers.

**Third:** Hold up your thumb and first two fingers.

**Fourth:** Hold up four fingers with your thumb tucked in.

**Fifth:** Hold up all five fingers.

**Sixth:** Hold up three fingers with your thumb and pinky touching.

# MY FAVORITE CLASS IS _ _ _ _ _.
## (MATH, HISTORY, READING, SCIENCE)

**My:** Place your palm to your chest.

**Favorite:** Tap your middle finger on your chin.

**Class:** Form the letter "C" sign with both hands in front of your chest with your palms facing away from you. Then draw a circle with your hands until your palms are facing you.

 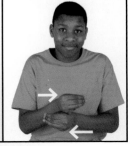 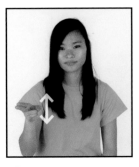

**Math:** Form the letter "M" sign with both hands. Then cross your hands in front of you two times.

**History:** Form the letter "H" sign, and then shake your fingers up and down twice.

**Reading:** Form the letter "V" sign with one hand. Then sweep your fingers down across the palm of your other hand two times.

**Science:** First form the letter "A" sign with both hands. Then hold out both thumbs and circle your hands in front of you toward your chest.

# THAT TEST WAS _ _ _ _ _. (HARD, EASY)

**That:** Point to the side.

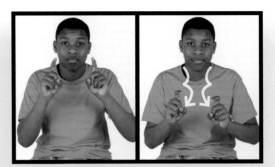

**Test:** Start with first finger on both hands pointing up. Then form the letter "X" sign two times with both hands as you bring them down in front of you.

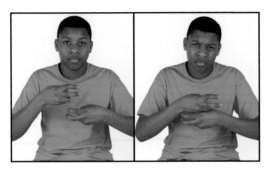

**Hard:** Bend the first two fingers on each hand. Hold one hand above the other, and then touch your hands together.

**Easy:** Hold both of your hands palm up. Brush the back of the fingers on one hand with the fingers of your other hand two times.

# OTHER SCHOOL WORDS

**Teacher:** Close your fingertips together and place your hands by your head. Then flatten your hands and bring them straight down in front of you.

**Book:** Start with your palms placed together, and then open them like a book.

# AROUND THE HOUSE

If you have a deaf friend, you might want to invite him or her to your house. Use the following signs to introduce your family, talk about your pet, and be a good host at home.

## HERE IS MY HOUSE

**Here:** With your palms facing up, move your hands in small flat circles.

**My:** Place your palm to your chest.

**House:** Place your fingertips together to form a roof. Then use your hands to form the walls.

## WHERE DO YOU LIVE?

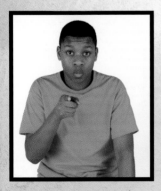

**You:** Point at the person you're talking to.

**Live:** First make the "A" sign with both hands. Then point your thumbs up and slide your hands up your chest.

**Where:** Point your first finger up and move it from side to side.

# I LIVE _ _ _ _ _ _ _ _.
## (IN A HOUSE, IN AN APARTMENT, NEARBY, FAR AWAY)

**I:** Point to your chest.

**Live:** First make the "A" sign with both hands. Then point your thumbs up and slide your hands up your chest.

**House:** Place your fingertips together to form a roof. Then use your hands to form the walls.

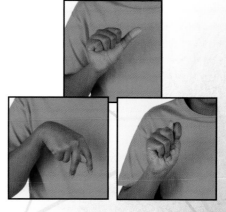

**Apartment:** Fingerspell the letters "A", "P", and "T".

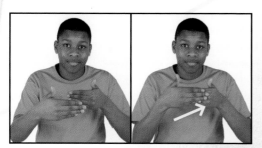

**Nearby:** Place both hands in front of you with your palms facing your chest. Your hands should be spaced apart. Then bring your outward hand in toward your other hand.

**Far away:** Point your first finger up and place your hand near your body. Then move your hand out and away from your body.

# THIS IS MY _ _ _ _ _ _ _ _ _.
## (DAD, MOM, GRANDPA, GRANDMA, BROTHER, SISTER)

**This:** Point to the person you are introducing.

**My:** Place your palm to your chest.

**Dad:** With your hand open wide, touch your thumb to your forehead.

**Mom:** With your hand open wide, touch your thumb to your chin.

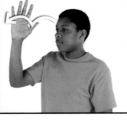

**Grandpa:** Make the sign for "Dad." Then move your hand away in two small arcs.

**Grandma:** Make the sign for "Mom." Then move your hand away in two small arcs.

**Brother:** Hold your thumb and forefinger by your forehead as if you're grabbing a cap. Then point your fingers in opposite directions and place your hands on top of each other.

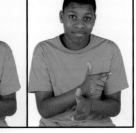

**Sister:** Slide your thumb across your cheek. Then point your fingers in opposite directions and place your hands on top of each other.

# I HAVE A PET _ _ _ _ _ . (DOG, CAT, BIRD, FISH)

**I:** Point at your chest.

**Have:** Bend your hands and bring your fingertips to your chest.

**Pet:** With your palms face down, stroke the back of one hand with the other toward yourself two times.

**Dog:** Pat your leg, and then snap your fingers.

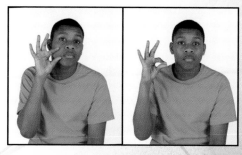

**Cat:** Pretend to grab and stroke imaginary whiskers on your face.

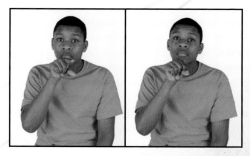

**Bird:** Form the letter "G" with your fingers and hold your hand at your chin. Open and close your fingers to imitate a bird's beak.

**Fish:** Hold your hand sideways with your palm facing toward you. Wave your hand from side to side while moving it away from your body.

## ARE YOU HUNGRY?

**You:** Point at the person you're talking to.

**Hungry:** Form your hand as if you are holding a cup. Put your hand on your chest with the palm facing inward. Then slide your hand down your chest.

## ARE YOU THIRSTY?

**You:** Point at the person you're talking to.

**Thirsty:** Point your finger to your throat, and then slide your finger down.

## DO YOU WANT MORE?

**You:** Point at the person you're talking to.

**Want:** Place your hands in front of you with both palms up. Bend your fingers up as you bring your hands toward you.

**More:** Touch your fingertips together on each hand. Then bring your hands together in front of you.

# I WANT TO EAT _ _ _ _ _.
## (HOT DOG, HAMBURGER, PIZZA, FRUIT, ICE CREAM)

**I:** Point at your chest.

**Want:** Place your hands in front of you with both palms up. Bend your fingers up as you bring your hands toward you.

**Eat:** Touch your fingertips together, and then bring your hand to your mouth.

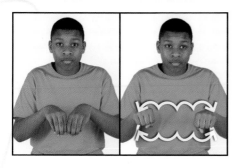

**Hot Dog:** Hold your hands next to each other. Move them apart while making fists two times like you're making sausage links.

**Hamburger:** Cup your hands together, then turn them over and cup them again as if you're forming a hamburger patty.

**Pizza:** Bend the first two fingers of your hand. Then draw the letter "Z" in front of you.

**Fruit:** Make the letter "F" sign, and then twist your hand at the corner of your mouth two times.

**Ice Cream:** Hold your hand and move it by your mouth as if you're eating an ice cream cone.

# I WANT TO DRINK _ _ _ _ _.
## (MILK, WATER, JUICE, SODA)

**I:** Point at your chest.

**Want:** Place your hands in front of you with both palms up. Bend your fingers up as you bring your hands toward you.

**Drink:** Cup your hand and tilt it toward your mouth, as if you are drinking from a cup.

**Milk:** Squeeze your hand into a fist two times like you are milking a cow.

**Water:** Form the letter "W" sign and then tap your chin.

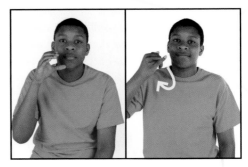

**Juice:** First make the "Drink" sign. Then form the letter "J" sign near your mouth.

**Soda:** Make the "O" sign with one hand. Bend the middle finger of the other hand and place it inside the "O". Then raise up that hand and flatten your fingers. Finally, bring your palm down on top of your other hand.

# THIS TASTES GOOD.

**This:** Point to object.

**Tastes:** Place your middle finger to your lips.

**Good:** Start with the "Thank You" sign. Then bring your hand down to rest in the palm of your other hand.

# PLEASE PASS THE _ _ _ _ _.
## (BUTTER, SALT, PEPPER)

 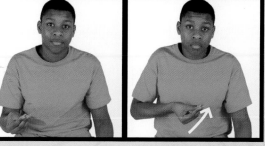

**Please:** Place your palm on your chest and move it in a circle.

**Pass:** Reach your hand out from your body and make a flattened "O" sign with your hand. Then bring your hand close to your chest.

**Butter:** Slide the first two fingers of one hand across the palm of your other hand. Do this two times.

**Salt:** Make the "U" sign with both hands. Wiggle the fingers of one hand to tap the fingers on the other hand.

**Pepper:** First form the letter "C" sign. Then move your hand as if you are using a pepper shaker.

27

# DO YOU WANT TO PLAY _ _ _ _ _?
## (BASEBALL, BASKETBALL, FOOTBALL, HOCKEY)

**You:** Point at the person you're talking to.

**Want:** Place your hands in front of you with both palms up. Bend your fingers up as you bring your hands toward you.

**Play:** Form the letter "Y" sign with both hands. Then shake your hands in front of you.

**Baseball:** Hold your hands as if you are holding a baseball bat. Pretend to take two small swings with the bat.

**Basketball:** Form the number "3" sign with both hands. Move your hands forward as if you are passing a basketball.

**Football:** Hold both of your hands up with your palms down and your fingers spread apart. Then bring your hands together and clasp your fingers together two times.

**Hockey:** Bend the first finger of one hand. Then slide your finger across the palm of the other hand two times.

# MY FAVORITE HOBBY IS _ _ _ _ _.
## (DANCING, MOVIES, RIDING BIKE, SINGING)

**My:** Place your palm to your chest.

**Favorite:** Tap your middle finger on your chin.

**Hobby:** Fingerspell the word "hobby" using the alphabet chart on page 7.

**Dancing:** Hold one hand flat with your palm up. Sweep the first two fingers of your other hand across your palm two times.

**Movies:** Hold one hand flat with the palm facing you. Place the other hand behind the first with the palm facing out and your fingers spread out. Then move the back hand from side to side.

**Riding Bike:** Make fists with both of your hands. Then move them in circles in front of you like you are pedaling a bike.

**Singing:** With one hand open, sweep it across your forearm in an arc two times.

## SEE YOU LATER

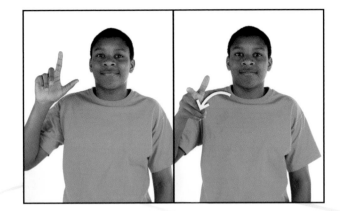

**See You:** Make the "V" sign, and then touch your middle finger to your cheek just below your eye.

**Later:** Make the "L" sign and hold up your hand. Then arc your arm forward.

## GOODBYE

Hold up your hand with your palm facing the person you are speaking to. Close and open your hand twice.

# Read More

**Flodin, Mickey.** *Signing for Kids*. New York: Perigee Trade, 2007.

**Heller, Lora.** *Sign Language for Kids: A Fun & Easy Guide to American Sign Language*. New York: Sterling, 2004.

**Warner, Penny.** *Signing Fun: American Sign Language Vocabulary, Phrases, Games, and Activities*. Washington, D.C.: Gallaudet University Press, 2006.

# Internet Sites

FactHound offers a safe, fun way to find Internet sites related to this book. All of the sites on FactHound have been researched by our staff.

Here's all you do:

Visit *www.facthound.com*

Type in this code: 9781429684262

Check out projects, games and lots more at
**www.capstonekids.com**

# Index